Henry Hudson

by Ruth Harley
illustrated by William Ternay

Troll Associates

Troll Associates,
Library of Congress Catalog Card Number: 78-18053
ISBN 0-89375-171-5
ISBN 0-89375-163-4 Paper Edition

10 9 8 7 6 5 4 3

Henry Hudson

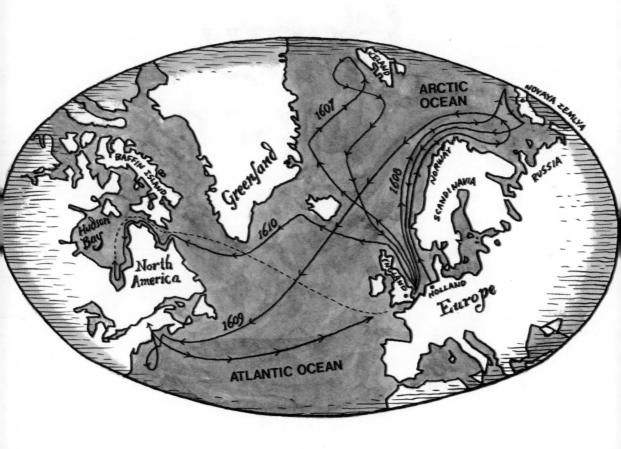

It was a Sunday morning in April, 1607. Outside St. Ethelburg's Church in London, an old man tapped John Hudson on the shoulder.

"Lad, weren't ye one of the crew that worshiped with us today?" he asked. "The men that the minister asked the special blessing for?"

"Yes, sir," said John Hudson.

"Will ye be aboard the *Hopewell* when she sails?"

"Yes, sir," answered John again.

"Ye be young to be going to sea! What can your father be thinking of?"

"My father is captain of the *Hopewell*," said John proudly. "He's Captain Henry Hudson! And I thank you, but I am not too young."

John touched his cap politely. Then he ran to catch up with his father, who had walked on ahead.

"Do you think I'm too young to go to sea, Father?" John Hudson asked.

Henry Hudson put his arm around his son's shoulders. "If thirteen is too young to go to sea, then I was too young when I first went. And so were your cousins and your uncles. Three generations of the Hudson family have either gone to sea or been agents for the Muscovy Company."

John nodded. He did not have to be told the story again. He knew that his great-grandfather and the famous explorer Sebastian Cabot had started the Muscovy Company to trade with Russia.

A few days later, on May 1, 1607, the small, square-rigged *Hopewell* set sail from southern England. Henry Hudson was in command, and John Hudson was one of the eleven crew members. The Muscovy Company, eager for trade, wanted Henry Hudson to try to sail across the North Pole to China and Japan. All other ships bound for the Far East sailed south—around the continent of Africa, then eastward across the Indian Ocean. This was a long, expensive journey.

Henry Hudson was a careful observer. He wrote down notes about everything he saw. One day, a surprised seaman called Hudson's attention to the ship's compass. "Look at that! What do you make of it, sir? Do you think the compass is broken?"

The needle of the compass was dipping strangely, but Hudson was not surprised. He knew that some scientists believed that the earth was like an enormous magnet. The nearer a ship came to the North Pole, the more its compass needle would waver back and forth. The *Hopewell* was now nearer the North Pole than any ship had ever been before.

As they approached the shores of Greenland, the weather changed. Strong winds tossed the tiny ship. The sailors saw large icebergs. Finally, the *Hopewell* could go no farther north. Ice was everywhere.

Hudson changed direction. Sometime later he sighted a group of islands north of Norway. Around the islands, the waters became calmer. The sailors were amazed to see great numbers of whales and walruses. "Whales Bay," as Hudson named this place, soon afterward became the center of the English and Dutch whaling industry.

11

Now the *Hopewell* headed back toward England. Hudson knew that there was no way for a ship to sail across the North Pole to the Far East. But he still had hopes of finding a short route to the Orient some day.

That winter, young John Hudson often found his father studying his charts. "The Muscovy Company wants me to try to find a route to China by going *northeast*," he told his son. He pointed out the route that he planned to take the following summer. He did not know that the charts were wrong.

For this trip, Hudson wanted to make sure the *Hopewell* would be ready for the rough, icy waters. He had the hull strengthened with sturdy planks, and he ordered thicker masts. He also took on extra food.

13

When the ship was ready for sailing in the spring, John Hudson was again one of the crew. Robert Juet was chosen as first mate. This time, Juet kept the daily journal.

The ship left London on April 22, 1608, and sailed north. Then it rounded the northern tip of Norway. After a few days, the men of the *Hopewell* found themselves in a strange world. It was the time of the short Arctic summer, and the sun shone 24 hours a day. The air was warm and balmy, but great masses of floating ice made sailing dangerous. Hudson recorded that the open sea had a greenish color.

Great flocks of sea birds flew above them. Below the surface of the water, the sailors could see whales, seals, and walruses. From the shore came the sound of growling polar bears.

On the morning of June 15, a seaman, alone on deck, suddenly called out, "Ahoy! A mermaid!"

Another sailor heard him, and hurried to the side of the ship. His eyes opened wide. "'Tis for sure!" he exclaimed.

The two men watched the creature in the water until it disappeared. Then they reported their experience to Captain Hudson, who entered the strange sighting in the log:

16

"This morning, one of our company looking overboard says he saw a mermaid. Her body was like a woman's, and they say they saw her tail, which was like the tail of a porpoise, and speckled like a mackerel."

In the early 1600's, many people believed that mermaids existed. The creature the men saw was probably a seal or a walrus, perhaps at a distance. Even so, that was an exciting day for the crew of the *Hopewell*.

17

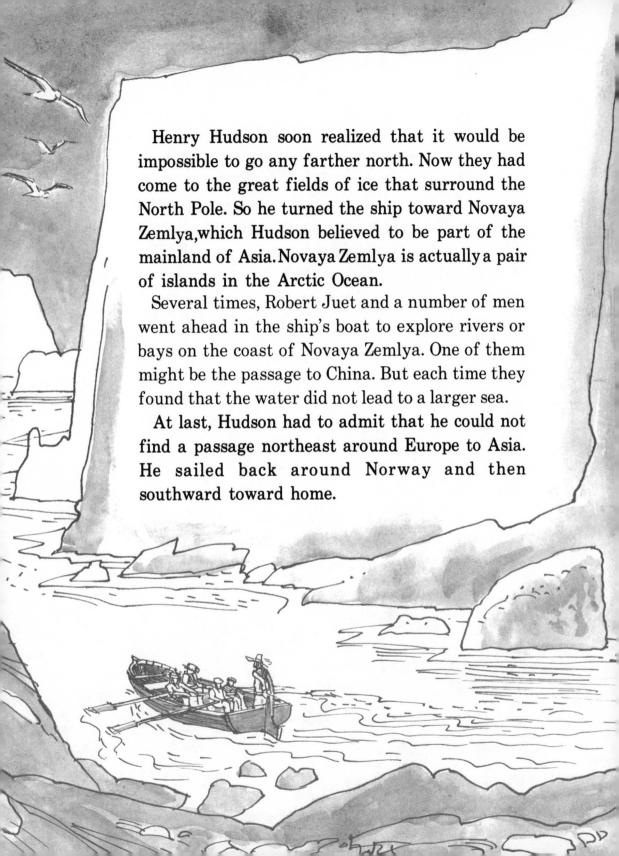

Henry Hudson soon realized that it would be impossible to go any farther north. Now they had come to the great fields of ice that surround the North Pole. So he turned the ship toward Novaya Zemlya, which Hudson believed to be part of the mainland of Asia. Novaya Zemlya is actually a pair of islands in the Arctic Ocean.

Several times, Robert Juet and a number of men went ahead in the ship's boat to explore rivers or bays on the coast of Novaya Zemlya. One of them might be the passage to China. But each time they found that the water did not lead to a larger sea.

At last, Hudson had to admit that he could not find a passage northeast around Europe to Asia. He sailed back around Norway and then southward toward home.

This time, the directors of the Muscovy Company were not pleased with Hudson's report. In two voyages, he had not found a shorter route to Asia. They did not plan to send him out again. But word of Hudson's voyages was spreading. In the fall of 1609, the Dutch East India Company invited Henry Hudson to come to Amsterdam.

While Hudson was in Holland, he learned of a new idea. He heard that there might be a Northwest Passage—an open waterway through North America—by which a ship could reach the Far East. This idea interested him very much. By now he was convinced that there was no *northeastern* route. But the Dutch still believed there was an Arctic passage. They agreed to furnish Hudson with a vessel, the *Half Moon*, and a crew. They instructed him to sail once again around the tip of Novaya Zemlya. If he could not find an Arctic waterway, he was to return to Holland.

Hudson quickly chose a mixed crew of Dutch and English sailors—18 in all. Even though Robert Juet had been troublesome on the last voyage, Hudson again chose him as first mate. Young John Hudson, now an experienced sailor, would also be a crewman.

The *Half Moon* was the type of flat-bottomed boat that Dutch fishermen used in shallow waters. She was not in top condition. And she was tiny—only about 60 feet long. In early April, 1609, the *Half Moon* sailed from Amsterdam and headed north.

22

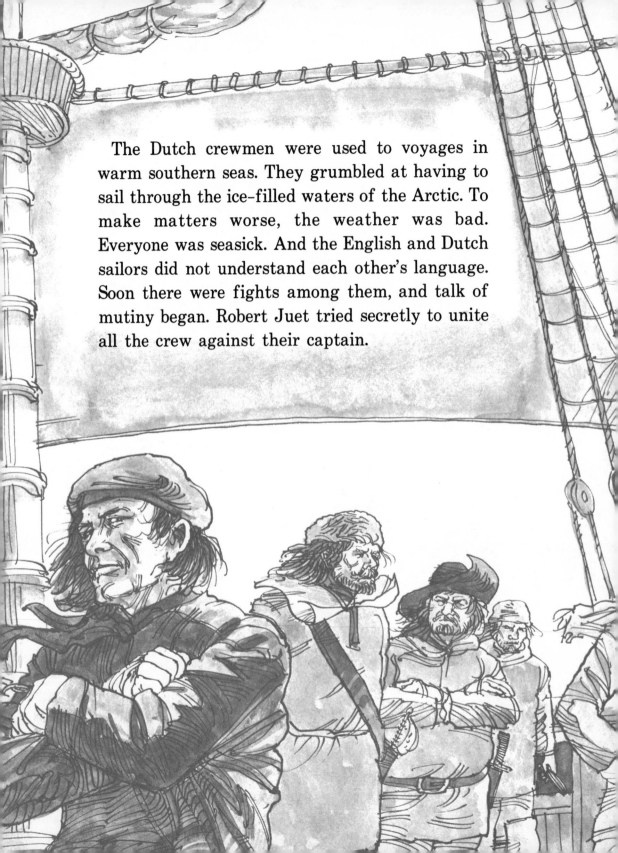

The Dutch crewmen were used to voyages in warm southern seas. They grumbled at having to sail through the ice-filled waters of the Arctic. To make matters worse, the weather was bad. Everyone was seasick. And the English and Dutch sailors did not understand each other's language. Soon there were fights among them, and talk of mutiny began. Robert Juet tried secretly to unite all the crew against their captain.

Hudson soon saw that he was not going to be able to complete this voyage. The weather was too bad . . . and the crew was in a dangerous mood. Discouraged, he decided to turn back toward Holland.

But then he had an idea. The summer was not yet half over. It would be a sign of defeat to return to Amsterdam so soon. Why not turn the ship around and look for the *western* route to the Orient? This was his chance to look for the Northwest Passage.

The men muttered among themselves. At least this would be better than sailing into the ice fields again. They agreed to change course, but only if they sailed southward, toward warmer waters.

Hudson would have preferred to look for the waterway along the northern part of North America. But he knew that Captain John Smith, the English explorer, believed there might be a passage near his colony of Jamestown, in Virginia.

So the *Half Moon*, helped by a favorable wind, headed south. On the Maine coast, the crew cut down a tall tree for a new mast. The land they next sighted was Cape Cod. The sailors who went ashore brought back grapes and flowers.

By the middle of August, the ship had reached a point south of Chesapeake Bay. Then the *Half Moon* turned and followed the coast back north. She sailed briefly into the Chesapeake Bay and up the Delaware River. But a passage to the west was not to be found here. Then the small ship headed north along the sandy coast of what is now New Jersey. It was September, 1609, when the *Half Moon* dropped anchor in the harbor of the river now called the Hudson. Here the water was clear and the fishing excellent.

On September 4, a group of Indians paddled toward the ship in canoes. They brought tobacco, which they traded for pieces of glass and beads. The following morning, some of the sailors went ashore. One man brought back dried currants, which Hudson found to be very sweet and tasty. The Indians had copper pipes and wore copper necklaces.

Looking at the Indians, Juet scowled and gripped his musket. "I don't trust them!" Several times during the journey along the American coast, Juet and other members of the crew had shot at Indians.

Hudson shook his head. "I think you're wrong," he said. "They are kind people. We must treat them well."

In the weeks that followed, the men on the *Half Moon* found that each tribe they met treated them in a different way. The Indians who hunted for a living were warlike. Those who fished or farmed were peaceful and friendly. They were eager to trade.

31

Then, on the morning of September 6, several sailors rowed out in a small boat to measure the depth of the water. Near nightfall, their boat was attacked. The Indians shot arrows—the sailors fired back with guns. One crewman was killed by an arrow, and two others were injured. The frightened sailors hid in their boat near shore and shivered through a rainy night. In the morning, they made it safely back to the *Half Moon*.

Other explorers had been in the area before, but none explored it as thoroughly as Hudson and his men. On September 12, the ship began moving up the broad river that Hudson called the "Great River of the Mountains."

This was the largest and most beautiful river any of them had ever seen. The autumn leaves were just turning to gold and crimson. "Here are fine timbers for ships, and wood for casks," Hudson wrote in his notes.

The *Half Moon* sailed as far north as present-day Albany. At one place, Hudson went ashore in an Indian canoe. He was treated kindly by a tribe of Indians living on the shore.

"The land is the finest for farming that I ever set foot on," he told his son. "And when the Indians saw that I wasn't going to stay, they thought that I was afraid of their bows. They broke their arrows into pieces and threw them into the fire."

Finally, when the river began to get narrower and shallower, Hudson realized that this was not the Northwest Passage after all. He decided it was time to head back. Winter would soon come.

But Hudson was uneasy. Would the rough crew, which had threatened mutiny, be willing to go back to Holland? Many of the men feared they would be punished once they got there. This may be why Hudson chose to land on English shores. Finally, on November 7, 1609, the *Half Moon* sailed into the harbor at Dartmouth. And from there, he and his son John went home to London.

The voyage had been a profitable one for the Dutch East India Company. Hudson had claimed the new lands for Holland. Within a short time, Dutch colonists and traders settled along the Hudson River. They founded New Amsterdam, which later became New York.

But the English were angry. Hudson had made discoveries for another country. The government ordered that any future trips must be for England.

35

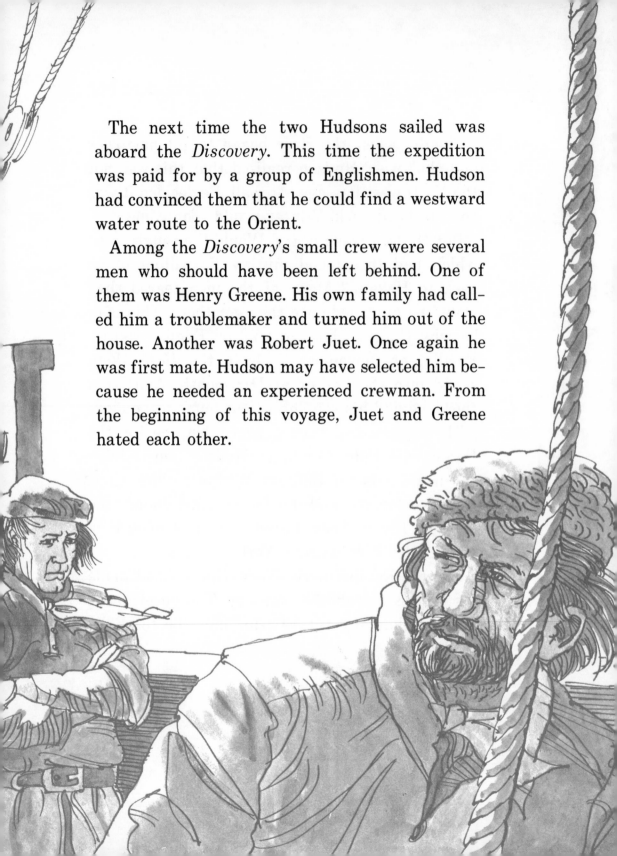

The next time the two Hudsons sailed was aboard the *Discovery*. This time the expedition was paid for by a group of Englishmen. Hudson had convinced them that he could find a westward water route to the Orient.

Among the *Discovery*'s small crew were several men who should have been left behind. One of them was Henry Greene. His own family had called him a troublemaker and turned him out of the house. Another was Robert Juet. Once again he was first mate. Hudson may have selected him because he needed an experienced crewman. From the beginning of this voyage, Juet and Greene hated each other.

The *Discovery* set sail on April 17, 1610, and headed northwest. Fog and bad weather forced the ship to land for two miserable weeks at Iceland, where Henry Greene lost no time in picking a fight with the ship's doctor. Juet saw his chance. He believed that the captain was giving Greene special privileges. So he began to stir up the crew against Hudson.

Slowly, the ship made its way through the ice-clogged passage now called the Hudson Strait—450 miles of water separating northern Labrador and Baffin Island. Hudson was the first man to navigate this strait.

In August, the *Discovery* reached a narrow channel and dropped anchor. Hudson sent three men ashore to climb a cliff and see what lay beyond. They rushed back to the boat in great excitement.

"An ocean!" they shouted. "Just beyond this channel is water as far as the eye can see."

"Thank God!" Hudson exclaimed. "We have found the Pacific Ocean."

What the men believed to be the Pacific Ocean was really a huge body of water—Hudson Bay. This inland sea lies in one of the coldest regions of the world. The water in the bay is frozen for more than nine months of each year.

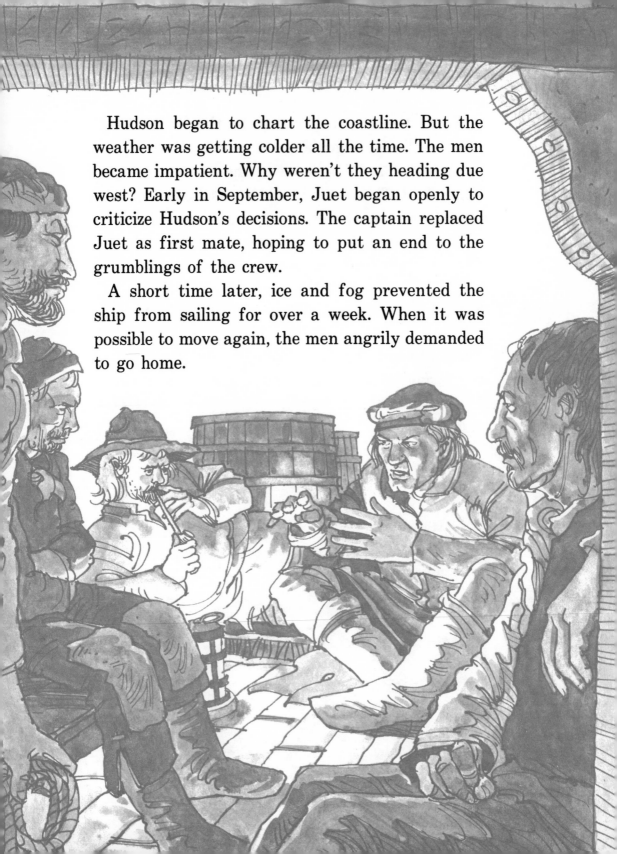

Hudson began to chart the coastline. But the weather was getting colder all the time. The men became impatient. Why weren't they heading due west? Early in September, Juet began openly to criticize Hudson's decisions. The captain replaced Juet as first mate, hoping to put an end to the grumblings of the crew.

A short time later, ice and fog prevented the ship from sailing for over a week. When it was possible to move again, the men angrily demanded to go home.

But instead of giving orders to sail, Hudson sent out a scouting party to find a good place to spend the winter. Finally, the ship dropped anchor on the south shore of the bay. By November 10, the *Discovery* was frozen in for the winter.

The men knew that the ship had left with only enough supplies for six months. They suspected that there was not enough food to keep all of them alive through the winter. But when Hudson put everyone on limited rations, the crew became even angrier. Juet and Greene fought constantly. Some men hid extra food, and everyone was frightened and hungry.

As the bitterly cold months passed, one argument after another broke out. Many of the men became sick with scurvy. Some of them suffered frozen feet. When one sailor died, the crew fought over his belongings. Food was almost gone. They even ate moss.

Spring came at last. Hudson now suspected that this body of water was not the Pacific Ocean. But still, he would not give up his dream. He headed the ship westward. Now mutiny was on everyone's mind. The men wanted to go home. They whispered among themselves that Hudson did not seem to care about anything but his dream.

One night in June, 1611, a seaman lay wearily in his bunk.

"Prickett," he heard a voice say.

"Aye?"

"Shhh. It's me, Greene."

Whispering, Henry Greene began to explain his plan. By now, most of the men were against the captain. They had decided to seize the *Discovery* and take command.

"Are ye with us or against us?" Greene asked Prickett.

At first, Prickett refused to go along. "We'll be hanged when we get home," he said.

"Better hanged at home than starved to death here!" was Greene's answer.

The next morning the men took the captain by surprise. They forced him, with his son John and seven men who were too sick to sail, into the *Discovery's* small rowboat. Then they lowered it into the water.

For several hours, the boat was towed along behind. Then, as darkness fell over the cold sea, one of the men on the *Discovery* cut the rope.

44

The return voyage of the *Discovery* was far from pleasant. Without Hudson as captain and navigator, the crew quarreled often about which direction they should take. Once they landed on an island and tried to steal food from Eskimos living there. Henry Greene and three other men were killed. Robert Juet died of starvation not long afterward.

The handful of feeble sailors that finally reached England swore that the mutiny had not been their idea. Juet and Greene, the ringleaders, were both dead. So the survivors were never punished.

The famous navigator was never found—nor were any of the men cast adrift with him.

47

In only four short years, Henry Hudson had made four voyages that greatly increased people's knowledge of the New World. His explorations proved that the long-sought northern passage to the Far East did not exist. It was his account of the beautiful Hudson River that led the Dutch to settle the Hudson Valley area. And it was Hudson's discoveries farther north that caused England to claim the land that is now Canada.

Even though Henry Hudson did not live to realize his dream of finding a short route to the Orient, he will always be remembered as one of the world's great sailors of discovery.